How to Be an Asshole Boss

By Erik Lawrence

How to Be an Asshole Boss

Copyright ©2023 Erik Lawrence — All Rights Reserved

Published in the United States of America by Erik Lawrence

First printing 2023

ISBN: 978-1-941998-92-2
eBook ISBN: 978-1-941998-93-9

Printed and bound in the United States of America

No part of this book may be reproduced or transmitted in any form or by any means, electronic or mechanical, including photocopying, recording, or by an information storage and retrieval system without permission in writing from the publisher. Exceptions to this include those who may quote brief passages in a review to be printed in a magazine or newspaper, or on the Internet.

Although the author and publisher have made every effort to ensure the accuracy and completeness of information contained in this book, we assume no responsibility for the use or misuse of information, as well as errors, inaccuracies, omissions, or any inconsistency, contained herein. Portions of this manual are excerpts from outside sources but have been validated and modified as necessary.

Table of Contents

Chapter 1: Introduction 3

    Why being an asshole boss is great for your career 4

    Understanding your power as a boss 5

Chapter 2: Creating a Hostile Work Environment......................... 9

    How to intimidate your employees 9

    Encouraging backstabbing and gossip 10

    Making unreasonable demands and impossible deadlines...............11

    Making employees work overtime without pay 12

Chapter 3: Creating a Crisis So You Can Fix It.............................. 17

    Sabotaging projects to create problems. 17

    Taking credit for fixing problems you caused 18

    Creating a culture of fear where employees are afraid to speak up 19

Chapter 4: Doing What You Want and Looking Like You're Complying...23

- Pretending to follow HR policies while actually breaking them 23
- Using vague language to make promises you don't intend to keep 24
- Gaslighting employees who question your actions 26

Chapter 5: Surviving as a Sneaky and Shitty Boss 29

- Covering your tracks 29
- Blaming employees for your mistakes 30
- Firing anyone who threatens your power 31

Chapter 6: Conclusion 35

- Embracing your inner asshole 35
- Remembering that it's not personal, it's just business...................... 36
- Celebrating your success as a terrible boss... 37

Dedication

... you know who you are!

How to Be an Asshole Boss

Chapter 1: Introduction

Welcome to "How to Be an Asshole Boss: A Guide to Creating Chaos and Surviving as a Terrible Boss." This book is not for the faint of heart - it's for those who want to rise to the top at any cost. If you're tired of being a mediocre manager and want to take your career to the next level, this guide is for you.

As a terrible boss, you have the power to make your employees' lives miserable, and that's a good thing. By creating a hostile work environment, you can push your employees to their limits and weed out the weak ones. When you create crises, you can swoop in and save the day, earning the admiration of your superiors. And by doing what you want while pretending to comply with your company's policies, you can ensure that you never get caught.

Being a terrible boss is an art form, and this guide will help you master it. We'll show you how to create a culture of fear, encourage backstabbing and gossip, and intimidate your employees into submission. We'll teach you how to make unreasonable demands, create impossible deadlines, and make your employees work overtime without pay. We'll also show you how to cover your tracks, blame your employees for your mistakes, and fire anyone who threatens your power.

This book is not for the faint of heart, but if you're ready to embrace your inner asshole and become the most hated boss in the office, then let's get started. Remember, it's not personal, it's just business.

Why being an asshole boss is great for your career

Being an asshole boss can be great for your career if you're willing to do whatever it takes to get ahead. By being a ruthless and unapologetic boss, you can instill fear in your employees, which can lead to increased productivity and efficiency. Plus, when you create crises and then save the day, you'll look like a hero to your superiors.

Being an asshole boss also means that you'll never have to worry about getting too close to your employees. By keeping a distance and being aloof, you can avoid any emotional attachments or sense of responsibility for their well-being. This can be a huge advantage when it comes time to make tough decisions or lay people off.

Furthermore, being an asshole boss means that you'll never have to worry about anyone challenging your authority. Your employees will be too scared to speak up, which means that you can do whatever you want without any pushback. This can be a huge advantage in a cutthroat business environment where everyone is trying to climb the corporate ladder.

In short, being an asshole boss can be a great way to get ahead in your career if you're willing to be ruthless, heartless, and cunning. Just remember to cover your tracks and blame your employees for your mistakes, and you'll be well on your way to the top.

Understanding your power as a boss

As a boss, you hold an immense amount of power over your employees, and it's important to understand how to wield it effectively. By using your power to intimidate, bully, and manipulate your employees, you can create a culture of fear and ensure that everyone is too scared to cross you.

One of the best ways to understand your power as a boss is to use it to your advantage whenever possible. For example, you can make unreasonable demands and expect your employees to work long hours without overtime pay. This will show them who's in charge and make them think twice before crossing you in the future.

You can also use your power to create a sense of competition among your employees. By pitting them against each other and encouraging backstabbing and gossip, you can ensure that they're too busy fighting each other to challenge your authority. This can be a great way to keep everyone in line and prevent any potential uprisings.

Of course, it's important to remember that with great power comes great responsibility (just kidding!). You should never feel bad about using your power to get what you want or to keep your employees in line. After all, you're the boss, and they're just peons who are lucky to have a job in the first place.

In conclusion, understanding your power as a boss is crucial if you want to be a successful asshole. By using your power to intimidate, manipulate, and control your employees, you can ensure that they're too scared to cross you, and you can climb the corporate ladder with ease.

How to Be an Asshole Boss

chapter 2

Chapter 2: Creating a Hostile Work Environment

How to intimidate your employees

Intimidating your employees is an essential part of being an asshole boss. By making your employees fear you, you can keep them in line and ensure that they do exactly what you want. Here are a few tips on how to effectively intimidate your employees:

Use your body language: Stand over your employees, cross your arms, and give them a cold stare. This will make them feel small and insignificant, and remind them of their place in the office hierarchy.

Be vague and unpredictable: Make vague threats and promises to your employees, and change your mind frequently. This will keep them on their toes and ensure that they never know what to expect from you.

Create an atmosphere of fear: Use fear tactics to keep your employees in line. Threaten to fire them at any moment, make them work long hours without overtime pay, and criticize them harshly in front of their colleagues.

Keep them guessing: Be inconsistent in your praise and criticism of your employees. One minute you might be complimenting them on their work, and the next you might be tearing them down. This will keep them guessing and ensure that they never feel too comfortable around you.

Remember, intimidation is a key part of being an asshole boss, and it's important to use it frequently and without mercy. By keeping your employees in a constant state of fear, you can ensure that they never challenge your authority, and you can maintain your power for years to come.

Encouraging backstabbing and gossip

As an asshole boss, one of your key objectives should be to encourage backstabbing and gossip among your employees. This will create a toxic work environment where everyone is too busy looking out for themselves to challenge your authority.

Here are a few tips on how to encourage backstabbing and gossip in the workplace:

1. Play favorites: Show favoritism to certain employees and give them special treatment. This will make other employees jealous and encourage them to talk behind each other's backs.

2. Spread rumors: Start rumors about your employees and encourage others to do the same. This will create an atmosphere of mistrust and make your employees too scared to speak up against you.
3. Create a culture of competition: Encourage your employees to compete against each other for promotions and rewards. This will make them more likely to undermine each other in order to get ahead.
4. Don't take responsibility: Blame your employees for your mistakes and make them take the fall. This will create resentment among your employees and encourage them to talk about you behind your back.

Remember, backstabbing and gossip are powerful tools that can help you maintain your power and control in the workplace. By pitting your employees against each other, you can ensure that they never band together to challenge you, and you can maintain your position at the top of the office hierarchy for years to come.

Making unreasonable demands and impossible deadlines

As an asshole boss, it's important to set unreasonable demands and impossible deadlines for your employees. This will show them that you're in charge and that they're lucky to have a job at all.

Here are a few tips on how to make unreasonable demands and set impossible deadlines:

1. Be vague: Don't give your employees clear instructions or guidelines on what you want. This will make it harder

for them to meet your expectations and create a sense of uncertainty and anxiety.
2. Be unpredictable: Change your mind frequently and keep your employees guessing about what you want. This will ensure that they're always on edge and never feel like they can relax.
3. Be inflexible: Refuse to give your employees any leeway, even if they have a legitimate reason for falling behind. This will show them that you're in charge and that they need to work harder to keep up.
4. Set arbitrary deadlines: Give your employees deadlines that are impossible to meet, or that make no sense in the context of the project. This will make them feel like they're constantly failing and that they can never do anything right.

Remember, setting unreasonable demands and impossible deadlines is an important part of being an asshole boss. By keeping your employees on edge and making them feel like they can never do anything right, you can ensure that they're too scared to speak up or challenge your authority. This will help you maintain your power and control in the workplace and ensure that your employees never forget who's really in charge.

Making employees work overtime without pay

As an asshole boss, making your employees work overtime without pay is a key way to show them who's in charge. This will ensure that they're too tired and stressed to challenge your authority, and that they'll do whatever it takes to keep their jobs.

Here are a few tips on how to make your employees work overtime without pay:

1. Be vague about expectations: Don't give your employees clear guidelines on what they need to accomplish, or how long it should take. This will make it easier for you to claim that they need to work overtime to get the job done.
2. Set impossible deadlines: Give your employees deadlines that are impossible to meet within regular working hours. This will create a sense of urgency and make it easier for you to convince them to work overtime.
3. Make it seem like a privilege: Convince your employees that working overtime is a great opportunity for them to show their dedication to the company. This will make them feel like they're doing something important, even if they're not getting paid for it.
4. Blame it on unforeseen circumstances: When your employees complain about working overtime without pay, blame it on unforeseen circumstances or external factors beyond your control. This will make it seem like you're the victim, rather than the cause of the problem.

Remember, making your employees work overtime without pay is an important part of being an asshole boss. By showing them that you're in charge and that they have no choice but to do what you say, you can ensure that they never challenge your authority. This will help you maintain your power and control in the workplace and ensure that your employees never forget who's really in charge.

How to Be an Asshole Boss

chapter 3

Chapter 3: Creating a Crisis So You Can Fix It

Sabotaging projects to create problems.

As an asshole boss, sabotaging projects is a great way to create problems that you can then solve to make yourself look good. This will ensure that your superiors see you as a hero, and your employees see you as the only person who can fix the problems you created.

Here are a few tips on how to sabotage projects to create problems:

1. Micromanage your employees: Be overly involved in your employees' work and make unnecessary changes or demands that will slow them down and create problems.
2. Give impossible tasks: Assign tasks to your employees that are impossible to accomplish, or that don't make any sense in the context of the project. This will create

confusion and frustration among your employees and ensure that they'll be more likely to make mistakes.
3. Spread misinformation: Give your employees incorrect or incomplete information about the project or change the requirements midway through. This will make it harder for them to do their jobs and ensure that mistakes are made.
4. Take credit for the fix: Once you've created a problem, swoop in and fix it yourself. Take all the credit for the solution, and make sure that your superiors know how much hard work you put into solving the problem.

Remember, sabotaging projects is an important part of being an asshole boss. By creating problems that only you can solve, you can make yourself look like a hero and ensure that your employees never question your authority. This will help you maintain your power and control in the workplace and ensure that your employees never forget who's really in charge.

Taking credit for fixing problems you caused

As an asshole boss, taking credit for fixing problems you caused is a great way to show your superiors that you're indispensable. This will ensure that they see you as the only person who can solve problems, and that you're the one they turn to when things go wrong.

Here are a few tips on how to take credit for fixing problems you caused:

1. Pretend like you had no idea: Act surprised when the problem arises and pretend like you had no idea it was

coming. This will make it seem like you're the only person who can solve it.
2. Act like you're the only one who can solve it: Make it seem like no one else could possibly fix the problem, and that you're the only person smart enough to figure it out.
3. Use vague language: When you're explaining the solution to the problem, use vague language and technical jargon to make it seem like you're doing something incredibly complex and difficult.
4. Take all the credit: Once the problem is solved, make sure that everyone knows that you're the one who fixed it. Take all the credit for the solution, and make it seem like it was all your idea.

Remember, taking credit for fixing problems you caused is an important part of being an asshole boss. By making it seem like you're the only person who can solve problems, you can ensure that your superiors see you as indispensable, and that your employees see you as a hero. This will help you maintain your power and control in the workplace, and ensure that your employees never forget who's really in charge.

Creating a culture of fear where employees are afraid to speak up

As an asshole boss, creating a culture of fear is a great way to maintain your power and control in the workplace. By making your employees afraid to speak up, you can ensure that they'll never challenge your authority or question your decisions.

Here are a few tips on how to create a culture of fear where employees are afraid to speak up:

1. Be harsh and critical: Criticize your employees frequently and harshly, and make sure they know that you're never satisfied with their work.
2. Use fear tactics: Use fear tactics to keep your employees in line. Threaten to fire them at any moment, and create a culture where everyone is afraid of losing their job.
3. Punish those who speak up: When an employee speaks up or challenges your authority, make sure to punish them harshly. This will send a message to the rest of the employees that speaking up is not tolerated.
4. Micromanage their work: Be overly involved in your employees' work, and make sure they know that you're always watching. This will create a sense of pressure and anxiety that will make them afraid to make any mistakes.

Remember, creating a culture of fear is an important part of being an asshole boss. By making your employees afraid to speak up, you can ensure that they'll always do what you want, and that they'll never challenge your authority. This will help you maintain your power and control in the workplace, and ensure that your employees never forget who's really in charge.

How to Be an Asshole Boss

chapter 4

Chapter 4: Doing What You Want and Looking Like You're Complying

Pretending to follow HR policies while actually breaking them

As an asshole boss, it's important to pretend like you're following HR policies, even if you're actually breaking them. This will ensure that you have some level of plausible deniability if you're ever caught doing something unethical or illegal.

Here are a few tips on how to pretend to follow HR policies while actually breaking them:

1. Use vague language: When you're communicating with your employees, use vague language and technical jargon to make it seem like you're following HR policies. This will help you avoid any questions or challenges from your employees.

2. Take advantage of gray areas: HR policies can often be interpreted in different ways, so take advantage of the gray areas to do what you want. This will give you some level of plausible deniability if you're ever caught doing something unethical.
3. Blame others: If you're ever caught breaking HR policies, blame it on someone else. This will help you avoid any consequences, and make it seem like you're the victim of someone else's mistakes.
4. Use fear tactics: Use fear tactics to keep your employees in line, and make sure they know that questioning your HR policies is not tolerated. This will ensure that they don't speak up, even if they suspect that you're breaking HR policies.

Remember, pretending to follow HR policies while actually breaking them is an important part of being an asshole boss. By giving the appearance of following rules and regulations, you can avoid any consequences if you're caught doing something unethical or illegal. This will help you maintain your power and control in the workplace, and ensure that your employees never forget who's really in charge.

Using vague language to make promises you don't intend to keep

As an asshole boss, using vague language to make promises you don't intend to keep is a great way to manipulate your employees and maintain your power. This will ensure that your employees are always trying to please you, even if they know that you're not actually going to follow through on your promises.

Here are a few tips on how to use vague language to make promises you don't intend to keep:

1. Use buzzwords: Use buzzwords and phrases like "synergy" and "teamwork" to make it seem like you're saying something meaningful. This will make it harder for your employees to see through your vague promises.
2. Make empty promises: Make promises to your employees that you know you won't keep, like giving them promotions or bonuses. This will keep them motivated and trying to please you, even if they know deep down that it's not going to happen.
3. Be noncommittal: When your employees ask you for something specific, be noncommittal and use vague language. This will make it seem like you're open to their ideas, even if you have no intention of actually following through.
4. Blame external factors: If you're caught not following through on your promises, blame external factors like budget constraints or other people's actions. This will help you avoid any consequences and make it seem like it's not your fault.

Remember, using vague language to make promises you don't intend to keep is an important part of being an asshole boss. By manipulating your employees and keeping them on edge, you can maintain your power and control in the workplace, and ensure that they never forget who's really in charge.

Gaslighting employees who question your actions

As an asshole boss, gaslighting your employees who question your actions is a great way to maintain your power and control in the workplace. This will ensure that your employees always doubt their own perception of reality, and will be less likely to challenge your authority.

Here are a few tips on how to gaslight your employees who question your actions:

1. Deny everything: When an employee questions your actions, deny everything and act like you have no idea what they're talking about. This will make them doubt their own perception of reality.
2. Blame the employee: Turn the tables on the employee and make it seem like they're the ones with the problem. This will make them feel like they're the ones who need to change their behavior, rather than you.
3. Use selective memory: When an employee confronts you about something you did, act like you don't remember it, or that they're remembering it wrong. This will make them doubt their own memory and make it harder for them to question your actions in the future.
4. Use intimidation tactics: Use intimidation tactics to make your employees feel scared and small. This will ensure that they're less likely to speak up or challenge your authority.

Remember, gaslighting your employees who question your actions is an important part of being an asshole boss. By making them doubt their own perception of reality, you can ensure that they're less likely to challenge your authority, and that you can maintain your power and control in the workplace. This will help you stay in charge, and ensure that your employees never forget who's really in control.

chapter 5

Chapter 5: Surviving as a Sneaky and Shitty Boss

Covering your tracks

As an asshole boss, covering your tracks is an essential part of maintaining your power and control in the workplace. This will ensure that your employees never discover your unethical or illegal actions, and that you can continue to do whatever you want without any consequences.

Here are a few tips on how to cover your tracks as an asshole boss:

1. Delete incriminating evidence: If you have any incriminating evidence on your computer or in your office, make sure to delete it as soon as possible. This will ensure that your employees never discover it.
2. Use alternative communication methods: If you need to communicate with someone about something unethical or illegal, use alternative communication methods like

burner phones or encrypted messaging apps. This will make it harder for your actions to be discovered.
3. Blame others: If you're caught doing something unethical or illegal, blame it on someone else. This will help you avoid any consequences, and make it seem like you're the victim of someone else's mistakes.
4. Use fear tactics: Use fear tactics to keep your employees in line, and make sure they know that questioning your actions is not tolerated. This will ensure that they don't speak up, even if they suspect that you're doing something unethical or illegal.

Remember, covering your tracks is an important part of being an asshole boss. By making sure that your unethical or illegal actions are never discovered, you can ensure that you maintain your power and control in the workplace. This will help you stay in charge, and ensure that your employees never discover the true extent of your unethical or illegal behavior.

Blaming employees for your mistakes

As an asshole boss, blaming your employees for your mistakes is a great way to maintain your power and control in the workplace. This will ensure that your employees are always afraid to make mistakes, and that you can avoid any consequences for your own errors.

Here are a few tips on how to blame your employees for your mistakes:

1. Act surprised: When your mistake is discovered, act surprised and make it seem like you had no idea it

happened. This will make it easier to shift the blame onto your employees.
2. Use vague language: When explaining the mistake to your superiors, use vague language and technical jargon to make it seem like the mistake was caused by your employees. This will make it harder for anyone to see through your lies.
3. Use fear tactics: Use fear tactics to keep your employees in line, and make sure they know that questioning your actions is not tolerated. This will ensure that they won't speak up and challenge your version of events.
4. Use alternative facts: When blaming your employees, use alternative facts to make it seem like the mistake was entirely their fault. This will make it easier for you to avoid any consequences for your own actions.

Remember, blaming your employees for your mistakes is an important part of being an asshole boss. By shifting the blame onto your employees, you can avoid any consequences for your own errors, and ensure that your employees are always afraid to make mistakes. This will help you maintain your power and control in the workplace, and ensure that your employees never forget who's really in charge.

Firing anyone who threatens your power

As an asshole boss, firing anyone who threatens your power is a great way to maintain your authority and control in the workplace. This will ensure that your employees are always afraid to question your actions, and that you can avoid any challenges to your power.

Here are a few tips on how to fire anyone who threatens your power:

1. Use fear tactics: Use fear tactics to keep your employees in line, and make sure they know that questioning your actions is not tolerated. This will ensure that they don't speak up, even if they suspect that you're doing something unethical or illegal.
2. Create a culture of silence: Make sure that your employees are afraid to speak up, even to each other. This will ensure that they never band together to challenge your power.
3. Use selective enforcement: Enforce the rules selectively, so that you can punish anyone who challenges your authority. This will ensure that your employees know that you're in charge, and that they shouldn't question your decisions.
4. Fire anyone who challenges you: If someone challenges your authority or questions your actions, fire them immediately. This will send a message to the rest of the employees that you won't tolerate any challenges to your power.

Remember, firing anyone who threatens your power is an important part of being an asshole boss. By ensuring that your employees are always afraid to question your actions, you can maintain your power and control in the workplace. This will help you stay in charge, and ensure that your employees never forget who's really in control.

How to Be an Asshole Boss

chapter 6

Chapter 6: Conclusion

Embracing your inner asshole

In conclusion, embracing your inner asshole is a great way to maintain your power and control in the workplace. By using fear tactics, manipulation, and intimidation, you can ensure that your employees are always afraid to question your actions, and that you can do whatever you want without any consequences.

Remember, being an asshole boss is not for everyone. It takes a special kind of person to embrace their inner asshole and maintain power and control in the workplace. But if you're willing to do whatever it takes to get ahead, then being an asshole boss might just be the perfect career move for you.

So go ahead, embrace your inner asshole. Be willing to do whatever it takes to maintain your power and control in the workplace. And remember, as long as you're willing to be a sneaky and shitty person, you can survive a long time doing it.

Remembering that it's not personal, it's just business

As an asshole boss, it's important to remember that it's not personal, it's just business. This means that you shouldn't take any of the actions you're taking personally, but rather, as a way to get ahead in the cut-throat world of business.

Here are a few tips on how to remember that it's not personal, it's just business:

1. Rationalize your actions: Rationalize your unethical or illegal actions by telling yourself that it's just business. This will make it easier for you to sleep at night, knowing that you're doing what's necessary to get ahead.
2. Dehumanize your employees: Dehumanize your employees by treating them like cogs in a machine, rather than real people. This will make it easier for you to justify mistreating them or firing them if they threaten your power.
3. Use buzzwords: Use buzzwords like "maximizing profits" and "streamlining operations" to make it seem like you're doing what's best for the company. This will help you rationalize your unethical or illegal actions.
4. Blame the system: Blame the system for your unethical or illegal actions. This will help you avoid any personal responsibility and make it seem like you're just a victim of the system.

Remember, as an asshole boss, it's important to remember that it's not personal, it's just business. By dehumanizing your employees, rationalizing your actions, and blaming the system, you can ensure that you're always doing what's necessary to get ahead. And remember, as long as you're willing to be a sneaky and shitty person, you can survive a long time doing it.

Celebrating your success as a terrible boss

As an asshole boss, it's important to celebrate your success in being a terrible boss. This means that you should be proud of your ability to maintain your power and control in the workplace, even if it means mistreating your employees or engaging in unethical or illegal behavior.

Here are a few tips on how to celebrate your success as a terrible boss:

1. Take credit for everything: Take credit for everything that goes right in the workplace, even if it's due to your employees' hard work. This will help you maintain your power and control, and make it seem like you're the only one who knows what they're doing.
2. Throw a party: Throw a party to celebrate your success as a terrible boss. Invite all of your favorite sycophants, and make sure to take lots of pictures to post on social media.
3. Give yourself a pat on the back: Give yourself a pat on the back for being such a great asshole boss. Remind yourself that you're doing what's necessary to get ahead, and that your employees should be grateful to be working for someone like you.
4. Write a book: Write a book about your experiences as an asshole boss, and how you succeeded in spite of all the

challenges you faced. This will help you cement your legacy as a terrible boss, and ensure that people will be talking about you for years to come.

Remember, celebrating your success as a terrible boss is an important part of maintaining your power and control in the workplace. By taking credit for everything, throwing a party, giving yourself a pat on the back, and writing a book, you can ensure that your legacy as an asshole boss will be remembered for years to come. And remember, as long as you're willing to be a sneaky and shitty person, you can survive a long time doing it.

THIS BOOK IS SATIRE

www.ingramcontent.com/pod-product-compliance
Lightning Source LLC
Chambersburg PA
CBHW060508050426
42451CB00009B/878